AWESOME SUPER SIMPLE HABITAT PROJECTS

SUPER SIMPLE

BACKYARD PROJECTS

FUN & EASY ANIMAL ENVIRONMENT ACTIVITIES

CAROLYN BERNHARDT

CONSULTING EDITOR, DIANE CRAIG, M.A./READING SPECIALIST

Super Sandcastle

An Imprint of Abdo Publishing
abdopublishing.com

To Adult Helpers

The projects in this book are fun and simple. There are just a few things to remember to keep kids safe. Some projects require the use of nuts or sharp objects. Also, kids may be using messy materials such as glue or paint. Make sure they protect their clothes and work surfaces. Review the projects before starting, and be ready to assist when necessary.

······················

KEY SYMBOLS

Watch for these warning symbols in this book. Here is what they mean.

NUTS!

Some people can get sick if they touch or eat nuts.

SHARP!

You will be working with a sharp object. Get help!

abdopublishing.com

Published by Abdo Publishing, a division of ABDO, PO Box 398166, Minneapolis, Minnesota 55439. Copyright © 2017 by Abdo Consulting Group, Inc. International copyrights reserved in all countries. No part of this book may be reproduced in any form without written permission from the publisher. Super SandCastle™ is a trademark and logo of Abdo Publishing.

Printed in the United States of America, North Mankato, Minnesota
102016
012017

THIS BOOK CONTAINS
RECYCLED MATERIALS

Editor: Liz Salzmann
Content Developer: Nancy Tuminelly
Cover and Interior Design and Production: Mighty Media, Inc.
Photo Credits: Allan Weissmann/Cesar's Way Inc.; Mighty Media, Inc.; Shutterstock

The following manufacturers/names appearing in this book are trademarks:
Delta Creative™ Ceramcoat®, Elmers® Glue-All®, Sharpie®

Publisher's Cataloging-in-Publication Data

Names: Bernhardt, Carolyn, author.
Title: Super simple backyard projects: fun & easy animal environment activities / by Carolyn Bernhardt.
Other titles: Fun & easy animal environment activities | Fun and easy animal environment activities
Description: Minneapolis, MN : Abdo Publishing, 2017. | Series: Awesome super simple habitat projects
Identifiers: LCCN 2016944666 | ISBN 9781680784398 (lib. bdg.) | ISBN 9781680797923 (ebook)
Subjects: LCSH: Habitats--Juvenile literature. | Habitat (Ecology)--Juvenile literature. | Urban ecology--Juvenile literature.
Classification: DDC 577.5--dc23
LC record available at http://lccn.loc.gov/2016944666

Super SandCastle™ books are created by a team of professional educators, reading specialists, and content developers around five essential components—phonemic awareness, phonics, vocabulary, text comprehension, and fluency—to assist young readers as they develop reading skills and strategies and increase their general knowledge. All books are written, reviewed, and leveled for guided reading, early reading intervention, and Accelerated Reader™ programs for use in shared, guided, and independent reading and writing activities to support a balanced approach to literacy instruction.

CONTENTS

BACKYARD
RESIDENTS

H ave you ever watched animals in a backyard? Maybe you've seen a squirrel clinging to a tree trunk. Or a butterfly flying around some flowers. These animals are part of a backyard animal **habitat!**

BUTTERFLY

SQUIRREL

We humans have a big effect on Earth. And it is not always a good one. Our pollution and high population wears on the planet. It has even made some animals **extinct!** Sharing our backyards with wildlife is one way to lend a hand.

BACKYARD ANIMALS

Many different animals live in our yards and parks. These include squirrels, chipmunks, robins, pigeons, raccoons, rabbits, worms, butterflies, and more. Some areas even have larger animals, such as deer and wild turkeys.

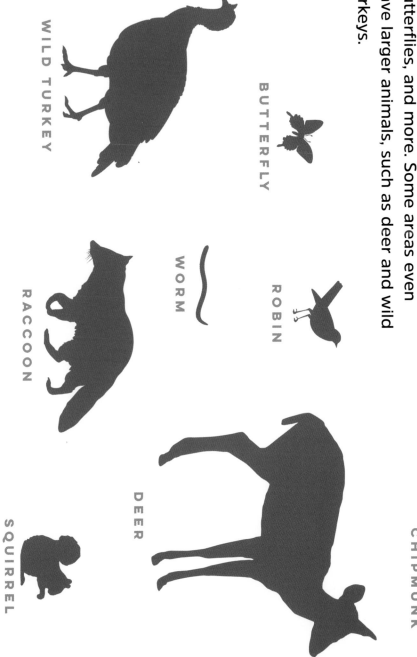

WILD TURKEY

BUTTERFLY

RACCOON

WORM

ROBIN

RABBIT

CHIPMUNK

DEER

SQUIRREL

BACKYARD
BASICS

What animals live near you? This can depend on where you live. Yards in different parts of the country have different kinds of wildlife. Pay attention to the animals in your area. Then, be a good neighbor to these creatures.

There are lots of ways to help backyard animals. You can grow certain plants or build feeders. Animals need water too. Ask if you can put a birdbath or small pool outside your home.

BACKYARD BIRDBATH

KEEP PETS INSIDE

One threat to backyard animals is loose cats and dogs. Their natural **instinct** is to chase and kill animals such as birds, squirrels, and rabbits. Keeping pets inside or in fenced areas is a great first step to helping local wildlife. It also keeps the pets safe from getting hit by cars or attacked by bigger animals.

HABITAT
FOOD CHAIN

Every natural **habitat** has a food chain. The food chain shows what each animal eats. When humans harm a habitat, they ruin the food chain's balance. This causes some animals to go hungry.

BACKYARD FOOD CHAIN

A food chain has several levels. The animals in one level mostly eat the animals in the level below. But some animals can be on more than one level.

The bottom, or level 1, of a food chain is plants. They make their own food from sunlight, air, and water. Level 2 of a food chain is **herbivores**. Level 3 is **carnivores** that eat herbivores. Level 4 is the top of a food chain. This level is carnivores that eat other carnivores. These animals have few predators.

4

3

2

1

LEVEL 1

BACKYARD PLANTS

crab-apple trees, flowers, garden vegetables, grasses, oak trees

CANINE CANNY

Cesar Millan is a famous dog **behaviorist**. He has trained dogs for more than 25 years. Millan came to the United States from Mexico in 1990. He has been working with dogs ever since. He stars in the television show *Cesar 911*. He was also the host of *Dog Whisperer*. His efforts to improve relationships between dogs and their owners have changed lives.

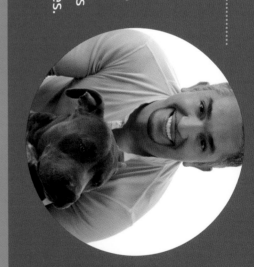

LEVEL 2

BACKYARD HERBIVORES

birds, chipmunks, earthworms, grasshoppers, mice, rabbits, squirrels

LEVEL 3

BACKYARD CARNIVORES

bats, birds, frogs, lizards

LEVEL 4

BACKYARD CARNIVORES

cats, dogs, hawks, owls

MATERIALS

Here are some of the materials that you will need for the projects in this book.

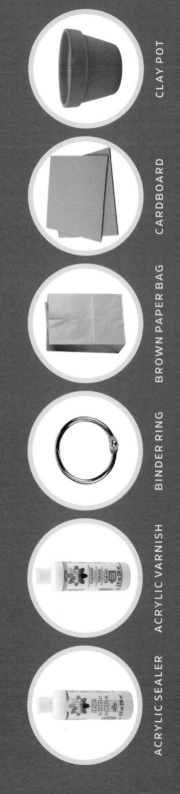

CLAY POT

CARDBOARD

BROWN PAPER BAG

BINDER RING

ACRYLIC VARNISH

ACRYLIC SEALER

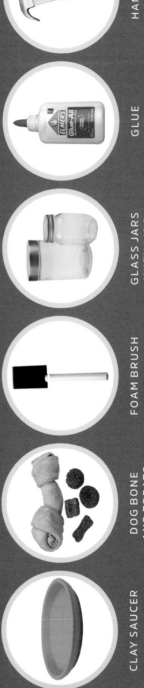

HAMMER

GLUE

GLASS JARS WITH LIDS

FOAM BRUSH

DOG BONE AND TREATS

CLAY SAUCER

MARKERS

NAIL

PAINT PENS

PEANUTS

PENCIL

PLANTS

PLASTIC CONTAINER

PLASTIC EMBROIDERY HOOP

PLASTIC SPRING

RIBBON

ROCKS

SAND

SEA SPONGE

SOIL

SPRAY BOTTLE

TROWEL

TWIST TIES

WATERING CAN

CROAK POT

MATERIALS: newspaper, clay pot and saucer, foam brush, acrylic sealer, paper plate, acrylic outdoor craft paint, water, small sea sponge, acrylic interior/exterior varnish, rocks

Frogs and toads are good neighbors. They eat a lot of insects. This helps keep pests under control. Frogs and toads are amphibians. They need water in their **habitats** to survive. Frogs spend more time in water than toads do. But they both lay their eggs in water. Frogs and toads also need sheltered places to hide in. This protects them from predators.

CREATE AN AMPHIBIAN HABITAT!

1. Paint the pot and saucer with sealer. Coat the inside and outside. Let it dry.

2. Pour some outdoor craft paint onto a paper plate. Wet the sea sponge and wring it out. Dip the sponge in the paint and dab it on the pot and saucer. Rinse out the sponge. Repeat with more colors. Let it dry.

3. Add words or other designs. Let them dry.

4. Paint the pot and saucer with varnish. Let it dry.

5. Set your croak pot on some rocks. This will leave room for the frog or toad to get in!

6. Put water in the saucer. Set it near the pot. Refill the saucer when the water dries up.

BUG BED AND
BREAKFAST

MATERIALS: wooden box, exterior paint with primer, paintbrush, insect habitat material (twigs, bark & pinecones), glue

Many insects help keep plants safe and healthy! They eat other insects that harm plants. And some insects pollinate plants. Pollination is when bugs carry pollen from plant to plant. This allows new plants to live and grow. Building a home for these critters is a great way to draw them to your yard.

MAKE ROOM FOR INSECTS!

① Paint the box. Let it dry.

② Collect insect **habitat** materials. Twigs, bark, and pinecones work well.

③ Spread glue in the bottom of the box.

④ Press the materials to the glue. Fill the box completely. Use small twigs to fill cracks until the box is tightly packed. Let the glue dry completely.

⑤ Place your inn outside. Watch to see who shows up!

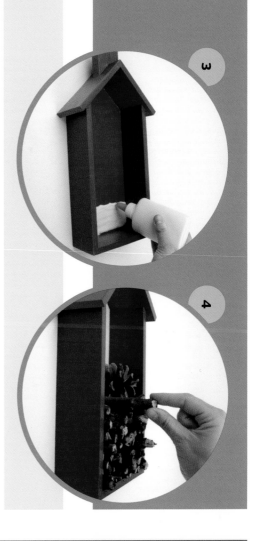

3

4

DIGGING DEEPER

Most insects will live anywhere that provides good places to lay their eggs. They often nest in small holes and cracks. These spaces keep insects and their eggs safe from the wind. Building bugs a secure place to nest is a great way to help backyard wildlife!

BEE BATH

MATERIALS: newspaper, large clay saucer, acrylic sealer, foam brush, acrylic outdoor craft paint, paintbrush, acrylic interior/exterior varnish, rocks, water

Have you ever eaten a bar of chocolate? Or smelled coffee? These are examples of foods that are made possible by bees! Bees are very important. They pollinate plants that humans like to eat. But bees need to drink water, just like all living things. Bees also bring water into the hive. This helps cool the hive.

LET BEES HAVE A SPA DAY!

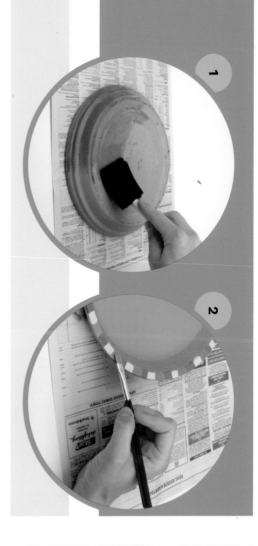

1

2

1. Cover your work surface with newspaper. Paint the outside of the saucer with sealer. Let it dry.

2. Paint the outside and rim of the saucer with outdoor craft paint. Let it dry.

3. Cover the paint with varnish. Let it dry.

4. Put rocks and water in the saucer. The water should not cover the rocks completely.

5. Place your bee bath outside near a garden. Keep it clean. Replace the water often so the bees have fresh water.

DIGGING DEEPER

Bees live in hives. They work together to survive. Worker bees are all females. They collect pollen and nectar for the hive to eat. They also clean and repair the hive. Drone bees are all males. They help with reproduction. The queen bee lays eggs. She also releases chemicals that direct the habits of all the bees in the hive!

PUPSICLE

MATERIALS:
dog bone, plastic container, water, freezer, dog treats

Ice is a fun treat for dogs to chew and lick! It helps cool them off on hot days. Some dog **specialists** even suggest freezing dog toys in giant ice cubes. This gives dogs something to chew on. It also gives them goals to reach. They want to get their toys back!

MAKE A COOL DOG TREAT!

1. Put the dog bone in the plastic container.

2. Add just enough water to cover the bone. Freeze the water.

2

3

3. Put some dog treats on the ice. Cover them with water. Freeze the new layer of water.

4. Remove the pupsicle from the container. Give it to your dog on a hot day!

DIGGING DEEPER

Did you know that dogs are related to wolves? Humans have kept dogs as pets for more than 14,000 years! But wolves have been around for much longer than that. These strong animals can live anywhere, from deserts to the arctic. Wolves and wild dogs can survive as long as there is food for them to eat!

SQUIRREL FEEDER

MATERIALS: plastic embroidery hoop, plastic spring, binder ring, twist ties, peanuts, ribbon

There are more than 200 kinds of squirrels! Some gardeners don't like squirrels. This is because they dig up flower bulbs and steal vegetables to eat. But many gardeners set up squirrel feeders. This gives the squirrels something else to eat instead.

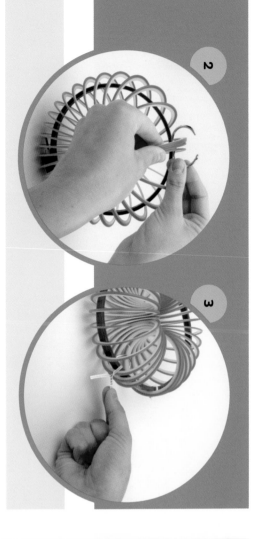

2

3

MAKE A SQUIRREL FEAST!

① Open the embroidery hoop. Remove the inner circle. Put the hoop through the plastic spring. Close the hoop.

② Use the binder ring to hold the ends of the spring together.

③ Spread the spring around the hoop. Use twist ties to connect about every fifth ring to the hoop.

④ Fill the spring with peanuts.

⑤ Tie a ribbon to the binder ring. Hang your squirrel feeder outside.

DIGGING DEEPER

A squirrel eats about one pound (0.5 kg) of food each week. This includes nuts, seeds, fruits, and insects. It can be hard for squirrels to find food during the cold winter months. So squirrels prepare for winter by burying food. They dig up this stored food in the winter. This way, they won't **starve** if they can't find fresh food.

BUTTERFLY
BUFFET

MATERIALS: newspaper, clay pot, acrylic sealer, foam brush, acrylic outdoor craft paint, paintbrush, acrylic interior/exterior varnish, plants, small rock, potting soil, trowel, watering can, water

There are many kinds of butterflies. Most of them need flowers and other plants to survive. Female butterflies lay their eggs on plants. Then the larvae eat the plants after they hatch. Adult butterflies eat flower nectar. Butterflies mainly use sight to find food. They are **attracted** to brightly colored flowers.

CREATE A GARDEN FOR BUTTERFLIES!

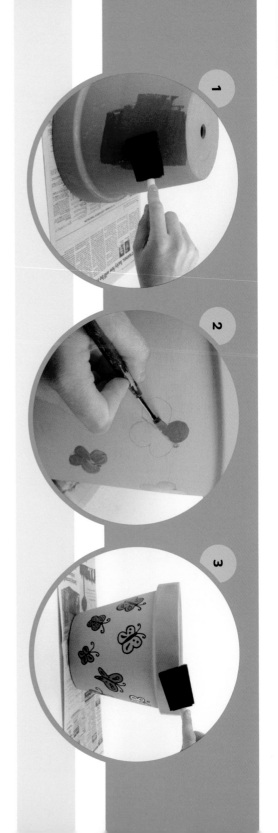

1 Paint the outside of the clay pot with sealer. Let it dry.

2 Paint the outside of the pot with outdoor craft paint. Use bright colors. This will **attract** the butterflies. Let the paint dry.

3 Cover the paint with varnish. Let it dry.

4 Have an adult help you **research** which plants butterflies are most attracted to. Choose different plants to attract different kinds of butterflies.

Continued on the next page.

BUTTERFLY BUFFET (CONTINUED)

5. Put a rock over the hole in the bottom of the pot. This prevents the soil from flowing out with the water.

6. Put potting soil in the pot. Fill it almost to the top.

7. Use the trowel to make a hole for each plant. Place the plants in the holes one at a time. Add more soil to cover all the roots. Press the soil firmly around each plant.

8. Water the plants.

9. Set the pot outside. Wait for the butterflies to show up and chow down!

DIGGING DEEPER

The monarch is a type of butterfly found in North America. Monarch butterflies migrate. During the summer, they mainly live in Canada and the northern United States. They travel south to Mexico and California when it starts to get cold. Female monarch butterflies lay eggs in the spring. The larvae hatch and soon turn into butterflies. After this happens, it's time to go north for the summer. Then the **cycle** starts all over again!

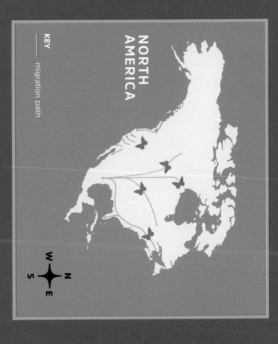

NORTH AMERICA

KEY
—— migration path

N
W — E
S

FALL MIGRATION
TRAVELING SOUTH

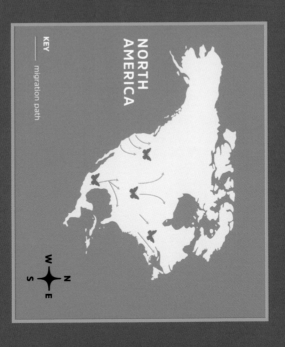

NORTH AMERICA

KEY
—— migration path

N
W — E
S

SPRING AND SUMMER
MIGRATION TRAVELING
NORTH

JAR OF WORMS

MATERIALS: large glass jar with lid, cardboard, hammer, nail, sand, small glass jar with lid, spray bottle, water, soil, food scraps (fruits, vegetables & grains), earthworms, plastic spoon, brown paper bag, markers

Earthworms are found anywhere that has moist soil. They usually live in dirt or leaf piles. Worms are an important part of any food chain! This is because they bring **nutrients** from the soil up to the surface.

MAKE A WORM FARM!

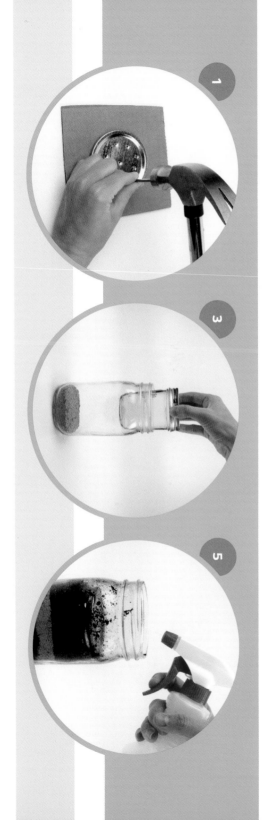

1 Remove the lid from the large jar. Set the lid on cardboard. Use the hammer and nail to pound some holes in the lid. This will let air flow into the jar.

2 Put a layer of sand in the large jar.

3 Put the lid on the small jar. Place the small jar in the large jar. This will prevent the worms from going where you can't see them.

4 Lightly spray the sand with water. Add a layer of soil to the jar.

5 Keep adding layers of sand and soil. Spray each layer with water after you add it. The soil and sand should be moist, but not soaking wet.

Continued on the next page.

JAR OF WORMS (CONTINUED)

6 When the jar is almost full, add some food scraps.

7 Add five or six worms. Find them outside or buy them at a bait shop. Put the lid on the jar.

8 Decorate the paper bag. Place the bag over the jar. Place the jar in a dark, cool place.

9 Remove the bag to check on the worms. Did they make lots of tunnels?

10 Keep and observe the worms for up to six weeks. Open the jar and add more food scraps once a week.

11 When you are finished, set the worms free in an area with a lot of dirt.

DIGGING DEEPER

Foods that are good for earthworms include fruits, vegetables, oatmeal, pasta, and cornmeal. Avoid giving them **citrus** fruit. Citrus fruit is toxic to worms.

Do you have a **compost** pile in your yard or neighborhood? That is a place you can put food and yard waste. The waste slowly turns into dirt. Earthworms are helpful to have in compost piles. When a worm eats food scraps, it breaks down the **nutrients** in them. Then dirt that is extra rich in nutrients exits out of the worm's tail end. This dirt is especially good for growing plants.

COMPOST

RICH SOIL

EARTHWORM

CONCLUSION

Human activities can cause a lot of harm to Earth and its animals. We need to work together to make the world better for the animals around us. This book is the first step in learning more about how to help the backyard wildlife in your area. But there is so much more to find out!

Go to the library to **research** the animals that live in your neighborhood. Or have an adult help you research these animals **online**. Learn how to keep backyard animals safe and healthy!

QUIZ

① What kinds of animals does Cesar Millan help people train?

② Where do frogs and toads lay their eggs?

③ **Citrus** fruit is good for worms. TRUE OR FALSE?

THINK ABOUT IT!

Even a small yard can be home to some amazing animals.
What animals have you seen near your house?

Answers: 1. Dogs   2. In water   3. False

31

GLOSSARY

attract – to cause someone or something to come near.

behaviorist – someone who studies the way a person or animal acts.

carnivore – an animal that eats mainly meat.

citrus – a fruit such as an orange, lemon, or lime that has a thick skin and a juicy pulp.

cycle – a series of events that happen over and over again.

compost – a mixture of natural materials, such as food scraps and lawn clippings, that can turn into fertilizer over time.

extinct – no longer existing.

habitat – the area or environment where a person or animal usually lives.

herbivore – an animal that eats mainly plants.

instinct – a natural pattern of behavior that a species is born with.

nutrient – something that helps living things grow. Vitamins, minerals, and proteins are nutrients.

online – connected to the Internet.

research – to find out more about something.

specialize – to pursue one branch of study, called a specialty. A person who does this is a specialist.

starve – to suffer or die from lack of food.